THE DRAGON KINGS PALACE

A Traditional Collection

KATIE CRACKERNUTS

A Story from Scotland

nce there was a King who had a
daughter named Anne, whose beauty
was so great no one noticed her step-
sister. Neither girl cared one smidgen about that,
and they loved each other as many real sisters do.

However, Anne's loveliness vexed the Queen, an
embittered jealous woman. It tormented her beyond
reason. "Why should Anne be so beautiful and my
Katie as plain as wheat-cake?" she repeatedly nagged
at herself. In the end, she sought advice from the
Henwife, a grisly old witch-woman if ever there
was one. Together they plotted against Anne.

Next morning, and early it was, the Queen said,
"Anne, my dear, go to the Henwife in the glen.
Ask her for some breakfast eggs."

Anne set off as she'd been bid, taking a crust of
bread from a shelf in the pantry to eat as she walked.

"Do you have some eggs for my stepmother, the Queen?" she asked the Henwife.

"Aye, I do. Lift the lid from the pot, Princess, and look in," answered the Henwife.

Anne took off the lid and was doused in a swirling fog of fetid steam. She saw nothing in the pot, no eggs at all.

"Ach, go home to your mither," grumbled the Henwife. "Tell her to keep the pantry door locked."

When Anne delivered the impudent message, the Queen looked annoyed but she made no comment about the Henwife's rudeness. Instead, next morning, and early it was, she sent Anne for eggs again. She herself shepherded the girl from the castle, checking first that the pantry door was locked.

So, an unfed hungry princess hurried along the road to the Henwife, until she saw some country folk picking peas in a field. Anne stopped to bid them good-day, and while they chatted she nibbled a handful of tender green peas, then carried off a pocketful to eat as she walked.

"Lift the lid from the pot, Princess," said the Henwife as soon as the girl arrived. And for a second time Anne lifted the lid to an escaping cloud of stinking steam. There were not any eggs. The Henwife shrieked, babbling wild words which lost their sense in high-pitched screams. Anne drew back, turning to walk away, and the Henwife calmed enough to yell, "Be off with you! Tell your mither a pot won't boil if the fire's away."

When Anne repeated the addlepated, extraordinary message to the Queen, she looked very grave and said, "We'll both go to the Henwife tomorrow, my dear."

On the third morning, and early it was, the Queen stood beside Anne when she lifted the lid from the pot and a sheep's head flew from it. Mercy! It fastened itself over Anne's bonny head.

Poor Anne! Poor Princess!

The Queen was overjoyed. The Henwife, wicked witch, crowed with glee. Her spell was successful.

But Katie was shocked and grieved to find her sister wandering about, heartsick and weeping. She took a fine linen towel and wrapped it about Anne's head. "We can no longer live amid such treachery," she told Anne. "We'll travel the world together and share our fortunes."

Katie led Anne from the castle and they traveled long roads to reach another kingdom. Katie found a refuge for Anne in an attic and work for herself in the castle's kitchen. "It's a strange household," Katie soon told Anne. "The King has two sons and one is sick enough to die. He will not wake, and no one knows what's ailing him. It is even more curious that whosoever sits to watch over the Prince each evening is never seen again."

No one now would watch over the Prince, although the King offered a peck of silver for the service. Then Katie offered, suspecting the Prince to be spellbound.

Quietly she sat by his bedside. The clock struck twelve. The Prince, who had been lying white and frail and still, silently rose and drew on his robes. Then, like a stick-thin shadow, he slipped from the room, treading softly down the stairs and out of the castle. It was as if he had been drawn away by an unseen power.

Katie followed the dazed Prince to the stables, where he saddled his mare. No sooner was he in the saddle than Katie leapt up behind, feather-light. She rode with him to the Green Wood.

The trees were laden with nuts, and, as they passed under them, Katie plucked handfuls from the branches, dropping them into her apron pockets.

Then they rode from the Green Wood to a fern-green hill where the Prince stopped to call out dreamily, "Open! Open wide and let the Prince pass."

"And his Lady behind him!" Katie added swiftly.

A door, green with turf and moss and ferns, swung open. They passed through it to a magnificent hall, glowing with lights and bustling with chattering, laughing, noisy fairy folk. "The Prince! The Prince!" their magpie voices shouted as they buzzed about him, dragging at his clothes, pulling his arms, demanding that he should dance with each one. Dance he did. He danced and danced until he fell exhausted to the floor. Fairies fanned his face, rubbed his cold hands, and pushed him to his feet to dance again. He danced until he fell once more, exhausted. Again and again they revived the Prince, and he danced until cock's crow.

Hastily, he mounted his mare. Katie sprang up behind him and they rode to the castle, through the Green Wood. Not once had the fairies suspected her presence in their hall.

Later, when the King anxiously visited his son's room, he was relieved to see Katie sitting by the fire, cracking nuts. "My son looks a little better," he told her. "Would you stay with His Highness yet another night?" he asked. "I will reward you with gold."

"Very well," answered Katie, and so she spent the second night watching the Prince. Again, on the stroke of midnight, he rose from his bed as if spellbound.

Again, Katie rode with him to the enchanted hall. Once more she entered with the Prince, and the fairies neither sensed nor saw her and she wandered among them freely. In a corner, a tiny fairy child played with a glittery silver wand, flashing it in swirls. Rustling and swinging, a fairy danced by, calling out cheerfully, "Be careful, Pillywiggins, of my bauble now! Three strokes from it and Katie's Anne will be as bonny as ever she was!"

Katie's heart swung right over with joy, and she bowled a nut across the floor toward the child. She bowled another nut. Then another! Fascinated, little Pillywiggins watched them coming. His hand stretched out. He dropped the wand to grab a nut. Katie grabbed it and hid it under her apron. There it stayed until she rode with the Prince to the castle.

And how she ran, scrambling up the stairs to the attic and her sleeping sister. One–two–three times she touched the sheep's head. With the last stroke it fell from Anne's shoulders. Anne woke to find her own bonny head.

The sisters' joy and thankfulness were marvelous, and then and there, they prepared to leave the castle; but first, Katie checked that her Prince was resting comfortably in his bed. And so the King found her and begged her to keep watch yet a third night. "Your son is more precious than gold or silver," she told the King. "I will stay for love of the Prince."

7

The third night was the same as the previous evenings, except that while the Prince danced, Katie found Pillywiggins playing with a wee bird. "Just look at that!" scoffed a passing fairy with a flutter of glittering skirts. "Nobody knows that just three mouthfuls of that birdie would break the spell binding our Prince. Just three mouthfuls and he'd be well again."

Uh-ha! So the Prince could be released from the enchantment. Katie rolled a handful of nuts toward the child. Bumping, clinking, they fanned out about his feet. His eyes shone and he clasped the bird to his chest, kicking the nuts with his feet…kicking, kicking. Katie waited for the kicking to stop and the rolling to stop, then she bowled her roundest nut. It bumped Pillywiggins' foot and bounced backwards. He grabbed it, dropping the bird. Katie whisked the bird up, under her apron.

At cock's crow, the Prince and Katie rode back to the castle where she plucked the bird and prepared it for the pot. Soon its savory smell filled the Prince's room.

He stirred. He became restless, tossing about in his bed. His eyes moved under their lids, half opened, closed again, then opened slowly, lazily. He sniffed and drowsily murmured, "I wish I could have a bite of whatever is stewing."

"And you shall," promised Katie.

He took a spoonful eagerly, and enough strength flowed through him to enable him to prop himself up on his elbow and say, "If only I could have another mouthful!"

"You shall," answered Katie, spooning broth and flesh into his mouth.

8

"May I have another?" he asked, wide awake and alert.

"You can have the potful!"

"Then I shan't eat it in bed," said the Prince, no longer ill and exhausted. His once-glazed eyes sparkled. His once-pale face now glowed with well-being. The spell was broken.

When the king visited his son, he found him sitting by the fire with Katie. Their heads were close together. They were laughing. They were cracking the last of Katie's nuts and sharing the kernels.

Of course, it wasn't long before the Prince believed that Katie was the most beautiful of Princesses. No one ever convinced him otherwise because that is the way of love. They were married, and it is said that Anne married his brother. And so the sisters shared their fortunes and…"They lived happy and died happy, and never drank from a dry cappie*."

The King's Son and the Magic Song

A Story from Africa

Once upon a time, high up in the African mountains, there lived a great king. He had many cattle which he loved, but his favorite was a silver ox with horns that curled across his forehead and a voice like thunder. This ox led the herd, and when he bellowed all the cattle followed.

During the day they grazed in the tall grass down in the valley, and at night they were brought home to a yard or kraal. The fence was strong and high, and there was always someone on guard in case of danger. The king and all his men slept in huts which spread around the kraal in a circle. So they were never far from the lowing of the cattle.

Now the king prized his cattle so much that he made one of his own sons herdsman. Every morning his boy took the cattle out to graze in the pasture, and at sunset he drove them back to the kraal. In summer the grass grew tall—higher than the boy's head, and so thick that he could not see through it, so he had to climb onto one of the great rocks that lay scattered on the floor of the valley. The rocks were as tall as a hut, and, although at the bottom it was cool among the shadows, on top in the fierce sunlight it was blazing hot. Often the boy grew tired as he watched the herds and longed to lie in the sun and sleep; but he dared not, for he feared his father's anger if he should lose an ox.

But one day as he watched, an old woman appeared out of nowhere.

She came and talked to him. He told her how he had always watched for fear the cattle would stray, and how afraid he was in case his father's enemies should come and kill him and steal the cattle. Then she pointed to a smooth, round stone—as large as the tallest hut that showed up over the grass of the valley. The boy was surprised, for he had never seen the stone before.

"Come," she said, "this is your stone. See, it is so smooth that no one can keep his footing on it or climb it. But you shall be able to. As you grow, the stone will grow with you so that you will always be able to watch all the valley, and no enemies will be able to hurt you, for they will not be able to climb it. But beware that you do not fall asleep on it, for then all your cattle will be stolen."

She also taught him a magic song:
> *Come, cattle, come; all you cattle come to me.*

It had such a bewitching tune that all the cattle that heard it followed the singer. Then the old woman disappeared.

So the boy became an excellent herdsman and none of his cattle was lost, for every evening he sang to them and they followed him to the kraal, and none strayed. Nor could any be stolen during the day, for he watched in safety from the stone every day.

But at last, on one very hot day, the boy fell asleep on the stone, and the enemy saw him sleeping, for they were always watching to catch him off guard. They crept down from the hills and drove off all the cattle. When he woke up, not one head of cattle could he find. And although he sang his magic song:

Come, cattle, come; all you cattle come to me,

they did not hear him. He wandered about the valley looking and singing until the sun began to set, and then he returned to the kraal, wretched and alone. When he told his father what had happened, the old king was very angry and drove him away saying, "Never come back unless you bring my cattle with you."

So the boy wandered back sadly to the valley and climbed onto his stone and lay there in the moonlight crying, for he had lost his home. As he lay there, someone touched him, and he looked up and saw the old woman who had given him the stone and the magic song.

"I know what has happened," she said. "You have slept, and what I foretold has come to pass—the cattle are gone."

"And I am driven from the kraal until I find them," he said, and cried again.

"Don't despair," she said, "but go to the chief who has stolen your cattle and ask to be his man."

So he got up and traveled all night under the moon, between the gray mountains, up and down by winding paths between the grass and the rocks, through streams and bushes, until in the morning, as the sun rose, he came to his enemy's kraal, and within he heard his father's cattle.

He entered the kraal and went to the chief and offered to be his man. The chief made him herdsman of his own father's cattle. Every morning he took them out to the grass, and every evening he sang to them the magic song and brought them home, and none strayed or was lost. He served the chief for many years until he was a man full grown. But always he thought of his father's kraal and pondered how he might take his cattle and return to his home.

At last the chance came. It was the time of the great festival, when the harvest was brought home. The women made the beer and filled the calabashes to the brim, then stood them in a row outside the kraal. Then on the set day, the men and women went out into the fields to gather the first ripe mealies, and the children went to get wood in preparation for the feast. No one was left in the kraal but an old woman and the king's son, who was in charge of the cattle.

When everyone was gone, he took a sleeping-herb and ground it into a fine powder. Then he went to the row of calabashes and mixed some of the powder with the beer which stood ready for the evening's feast. Then he waited until they all came back.

When the chief and his people returned, there was great rejoicing. A hut of green branches was made for the chief to sit in, and the first fruits of the harvest were brought to him. Each family brought an offering: mealies, yams or nuts, or whatever they had grown. The chief tied the leaves or a branch from each offering to his arms or neck. Then his wise men brought him a drink made of fresh herbs and water from the sea, and they gave a sip to each person as a sign that the feast was to begin. Then everyone ate of the new corn or fresh nuts or drank the new beer. Only the king's son did not drink but waited until they all fell asleep. And when the evening came and the moon rose, not a man or a woman or a child was left awake.

Then the king's son stood up and climbed on the wall of the cattle kraal and sang the magic song:

Come, cattle, come; all you cattle come to me.

He opened the gate of the kraal. At once the cattle rose up and walked straight past the huts and the sleeping men and out into the country, following the king's son. As they went, the silver ox with the curling horns bellowed loudly, and at his call all the cattle came from the East and the West and the South and followed the king's son.

And he went toward his father's kraal.

When his enemies woke in the morning they could not find one head of cattle in their kraal, nor in all the surrounding country. The old chief was sure that it was the king's son who had taken them away, and he sent all his armed men after him. They gathered up their shields of ox hide and their spears and followed the tracks left by the oxen. It did not take them long to get within sight of the king's son, for the cattle traveled slowly, and they were sure that soon they would recapture all the cattle.

The king's son was afraid when he heard his enemies moving on the mountains behind him, and he did not know what to do. He led the cattle down the mountain, along the banks of a little stream where the trees grew tall thick thorns with yellow flowers like small pincushions, and the wild figs had tiny fruit—and tall reeds covered the banks, and monkey ropes hung from the trees down to the rocks and water. And everywhere ferns grew, and the clear water raced between the stones, slipping from pool to pool and playing with the leaves and rushes; and the bright flies hung over the water in the little ladders of sunlight slanting through the trees. There the king's son hid his cattle in the bush, and sat on the grass under a fig tree to think what he should do.

But he could think of no way to save the cattle. And the enemies drew closer while the evening came on, and the shadows rose over the creek and crept up the mountainside; and the frogs began to croak and the crickets sang and everywhere was the humming of gnats and the buzzing of mosquitoes. As he looked over to where his enemies were, the king's son knew that in the morning they would come and kill him and take his cattle.

Then, out of the darkness, he heard the voice of the old woman.

"Do not despair," she said. "Your task is nearly done. Obey me and all shall be well. Go and kill a white ox, skin it, and cut the hide into ten thousand little white shields, and I will find you soldiers."

So he slew an ox and skinned it and made ten thousand little shields from the hide.

Then the woman called to the frogs who lived near the stream.

"Frogs," she cried, "will you take these shields and do as the king's son bids you?" And from all over the valley they croaked, "We will!"

So the king's son gave them the shields, and all night long he drilled them in the moonlight. When he called, "Woo-ooh," they rose up, shouting, with their shields held out in front of them; and when he cried, "Boo-ooh," they fell to the ground and lay hidden.

Before dawn he placed them in a long line of the mountainside where the enemy would see them.

As the first company of the enemy appeared, the frogs rose up together, raised their shields, and croaked, "Woo-ooh!" with a sound like thunder. It was so loud that the enemy fell back in terror.

"There are many thousand men across the creek," they said. "No one can stand against them."

So the chief sent a larger company, but they returned with the same tale. Then he went himself with all his army; but when he saw the thousands of white shields and heard the war cry, he, too, was afraid.

"It is better to lose the cattle than to lose our own lives," he said, and he ordered the whole army to return home.

So the king's son was safe. He thanked the frogs, gathered his cattle together, and journeyed toward his father's kraal. His father, the king, received him with great honor and made him chief of all his sons. He gave him a princess for his wife, and his life was long and happy. But every night the king's son sang his magic song and kept his cattle in safety.

THE FIRST SUNRISE

An Aboriginal Story from Australia

Long, long ago, in the Dreamtime, the earth was dark. There was no light. A huge gray blanket of clouds kept the light and the warmth out. It was very cold and very black. A great gray mass of cloud was very low, so low that the animals had to crawl around. The Emu hobbled, neck bent almost to the ground; the Kangaroo couldn't hop, and none of the birds could fly higher than several feet in the air. Only the Snakes were happy, because they, of all the animals, lived close to the ground.

The animals lived by crawling around the damp dark earth, feeling for fruits and berries. Often it was so hard to find food that several days would pass between meals. The Wombat became so tired of people bumping into him that he dug himself a burrow and learned to sleep for long periods.

Eventually, the birds decided they'd had enough. They called a meeting of all the animals. The Magpies, who were more intelligent than most of the birds, had a plan:

"We can't fly because the sky is too low. What we need to do is to raise the sky. If we all gathered sticks, then we could use them to push the sky up—and then we could fly up with the sky and make lots of room for everyone."

All the animals agreed it was a good idea, and they set about gathering sticks. The Magpies took a big stick each, and began to push at the sky.

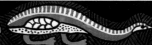

"Look, it's going to work!
The sky! It's moving!"

The Emus and the Kangaroos, the Wombats and the
Goannas sat and watched as the Magpies pushed the sky
slowly upwards. They used the sticks as levers, first resting
the sky on low boulders, then on small hills. As the animals
watched, the Magpies, pushing and straining, reached the
top of a small mountain.

"Munmuck, munmuck, at least we can walk about."

It was still very dark, but at least the Emu could straighten up, and the Kangaroo was able to move in long proud hops.

The Magpies kept pushing the sky higher and higher, until they reached the highest mountain in the whole land. Then, with a mighty heave, they gave the sky one last push! The sky shot up into the air, and as it rose it split open and a huge flood of warmth and light poured through onto the land below.

The animals wondered at the light and warmth, but more at the incredible brightly painted beauty of the Sun-Woman. The whole sky was awash with beautiful reds and yellows.

It was the first sunrise.

Overjoyed with the beauty, the light, and the warmth, the Magpies burst into song. As their loud warbling carried across the land, the Sun-Woman rose slowly and began her journey toward the West.

Now, each morning, when the Sun-Woman wakes in her camp in the East, she lights a fire to prepare the bark torch that she will carry across the sky each day. It is this fire that provides the first light of dawn. As she puts on her paint, the dust from the crushed red ochre colors the early morning clouds a beautiful soft red.

Then she takes up her torch and begins her daily journey across the sky.

When she reaches the western edge of the world, she extinguishes her flaming bark torch. Then she sits down and repaints herself in brilliant reds and yellows, ready for her journey through a long underground passage, back to her camp in the East.

So that is why, to this day, every morning when the Sun-Woman wakes and lights her early morning fire, all the Magpies greet her with their beautiful song.

THE DAY IT RAINED RAISINS AND FIGS

A Story from Italy

There was once a widow who was as witty and clever as her son was dull and stupid. The woman's brain was as sharp as a pinpoint, but although her son, Vardiello, was a good lad, his head was as empty as a drum. All the same, his mother adored him, and in her eyes he could do no wrong. It was just as well, because as you will see, things turned out well in the end, despite his foolishness.

Now the widow had a hen sitting on a nest full of eggs; about a dozen eggs there were. The eggs were due to hatch quite soon, so she watched the nest carefully for the first signs of cracking. But one morning she had to go out, and that meant leaving Vardiello in charge of things.

"Listen carefully, Vardiello," she said. "While I'm out, keep your eyes on the hen, and if she gets off

the nest and starts scratching around in the yard, be sure to send her straight back to the nest; otherwise the eggs will get cold and we'll have no chicks."

"Leave everything to me," he answered. "Don't worry about a thing. I'm not stupid, like some people!"

"There's just one other thing," said his mother seriously. "There's a jar in the cupboard which you must not touch. It might look as if it's full of walnut creams, but if you so much as sniff them, you'll be a goner."

"Just as well you told me," said Vardiello. "I might easily have eaten the whole jarful, thinking they were walnut creams. Now I won't even sniff them."

Having got everything straight, his mother picked up her basket and was off. Next thing—would you believe it?—the hen flapped her wings, got up off the nest, and began to scratch around in the yard. But Vardiello had his eyes open and was after her in a wink.

"Shoo! Shoo there, you silly old hen!" he shouted. "Go back! Get back on the nest."

Then what did the hen do but get flustered, excited-like. She squawked and flapped and rustled past him into the kitchen.

In he ran after her, waving his arms and still shouting, "Shoo! Shoo! Shoo!"

But he couldn't see her anywhere. He ran all around the house, then back into the kitchen. Then he saw her under the table, pecking quietly away at the breakfast crumbs. He stamped his feet. She went on pecking. He threw his cap. She went on pecking. Then his eyes spied the firewood piled into the corner, so he picked up a piece and threw it. The wood hit the hen on the head and she fell down dead.

"Oh, dear," he cried. "Now the hen is dead, and the eggs will get cold, and we'll have no chicks. Oh, poor me. Won't Mother be cross!"

He thought for a bit. Then, in a flash, he knew what to do.

"I know! I'll keep them warm *myself*!" So he ran out of the house and over to the nest where the eggs lay uncovered. Then, very gently, he sat himself down on the eggs.

Crunch, scrunch! Slish, slosh! What a mess of scrambled eggs that was! And you should have seen his trousers when he stood up!

"Now the hen is dead, and there won't be any chicks, and I've ruined my trousers," wailed Vardiello.

He felt so miserable that all he wanted to do was eat and eat and eat, to comfort himself.

"It's a pity that jar isn't full of walnut creams," he said.

Again he thought for a bit. Then, all of a sudden, he knew what to do.

"I know! I'll roast the hen! Better not to waste her."

So he plucked out her feathers and cleaned her and fixed her on the spit. He made a good fire, and when it was burning well, he began to roast the hen. Then he found his mother's best tablecloth and set the table; and when the hen was golden brown he put her, spit and all, on a dish in the center of the table.

Now the feast was almost ready. Only the wine was missing. So he went down the stairs into the cellar to fill a jug with wine from the cask. He turned on the tap and then—Crash! Smash! What a din! Vardiello ran straight up the stairs, two at a time, to find out what was happening.

The room was chaotic: chairs turned on their sides, tablecloth in a heap on the floor, broken dishes everywhere, and bounding out the door—a large spotted dog with the hen, spit and all, in its mouth.

Vardiello gave chase, but he was not quick enough. The dog simply disappeared. Well, what could he do now? Go home, of course. So he did.

When he reached the door, he remembered the wine. He had left

the tap running! He tumbled down the stairs and there was the cellar awash with wine and the cask empty.

Tears streamed down his cheeks as he turned and climbed slowly back up the stairs. It was too much.

"No hen. No chicks. Ruined trousers. And now no wine left in the house," he said. "Poor me. Oh, I wish I were dead."

Then he thought of the jar. He went straight to the cupboard, reached up for the jar and brought it down. He unscrewed the lid, and he ate and ate. He didn't stop until the jar was empty. For poison, it tasted remarkably good. Very much like walnut creams, in fact. Then he curled up under the table and got ready to die.

Presently his mother came home. She looked around her, astonished, dismayed. It was just as if a herd of cows had trampled through the house: chairs overturned, broken dishes everywhere, and her best tablecloth in a heap on the floor.

"Vardiello," she called, "where are you?"

There was no answer.

"Vardiello, are you stone-deaf?"

Silence.

Then she heard a low voice, sounding very sorry for itself.

"Mother, I'm down here, under the table. I'm a goner! I'm dead, stone-dead!"

"Why, Vardiello! What has happened?"

"I've eaten those things in the jar, the ones that looked like walnut creams, and as you said, I'm a goner!"

He told her about all the stupid things he'd done. But when he got up to the "brown things," she just laughed and laughed; and when at last she stopped laughing, she pulled him from under the table.

"You won't die," she said. "They *were* walnut creams. I only said that you'd be a goner to keep you away from the jar so you wouldn't

be tempted to eat them all—but that is just what you have done!"

But Vardiello would not be consoled. He moped about the house, as if the end of the world had come.

Next morning, to take his mind off his troubles, his mother gave him something to do. She handed him a length of cloth she had woven and asked him to take it to Naples and try to sell it.

"For goodness sake, keep your wits about you and don't let anyone cheat you," she said. "Don't believe everything people say. Especially be careful of merchants who talk with honeyed tongues. That kind of person can't be trusted."

"Leave it to me, Mother," he cried. "No need to worry."

So, tucking the roll of cloth under his arm, Vardiello set off for Naples. When he got there, he marched up and down the street calling, "Cloth! Cloth! Fine cloth for sale!"

Now quite a few people were interested, and they asked questions like, "What kind of cloth is it?" or, "How much of it have you got?" or, "What's the price?"

But to each question Vardiello gave the same reply: "I'm not selling to you. You're not to be trusted. You've got too much to say for yourself."

By the end of the day he had not sold the cloth, and as it was growing dark, he decided to return home.

On the way, he passed a derelict house, and because he was tired from so much walking, he sat down to rest on a nearby wall. He looked toward the house and saw the statue of a man standing in the courtyard.

"Good day to you, sir," he called. "Would you like to buy some cloth?"

No answer.

Vardiello smiled and slapped his thigh with delight.

"At last—at last—I've met the man I've been looking for," he cried. "A silent merchant! A man who can be trusted! Good sir, take this cloth. Examine it carefully and name your price."

Still no answer.

"All right, then, it's settled. I'll come back tomorrow. Same time. Same place."

Then Vardiello dumped the cloth on the wall in front of the man and went home.

Of course, it was not long before a passerby discovered the cloth and went off with his lucky find.

When Vardiello arrived home with neither cloth nor money, and told his mother about the silent man standing in the middle of the courtyard, she wrung her hands in despair.

"Oh, Vardiello! Vardiello!" she said. "When will you get some sense in your head? We'll be ruined; no cloth and no money either."

"Now don't worry," he answered. "I'm going to pick up the money tomorrow. It's sure to be there."

The next morning he set off for the derelict house, and when he

arrived, the man *was* there. He was still standing in the middle of the courtyard.

"Good morning," said Vardiello. "I trust that it is now convenient for you to pay me that small sum of money that you owe me?"

There was no answer.

"Now come on, sir, pay up, please."

Still no answer. Was the man deaf?

"Pay me for the cloth!" he shouted, stepping closer.

Then he saw for himself—there was no man there. It was just a statue!

He was furious. He picked up a brick and hurled it at the statue, hitting it right in the middle of its stomach. Lumps of plaster fell to the ground, leaving a hole in its stomach. Vardiello peered inside. It was hollow—but what was that large jar doing in there? And why was it filled with golden coins?

For once in his life he thought quickly! And before you could say "knife," he was home, clutching the jar of coins close to his chest.

"Mother, Mother," he called. "Come and look! See what I've found! Gold coins! Hundreds of them!"

"Oh, my clever, clever son!" she cried, hugging and kissing him again and again.

But then her face grew serious and she said, "Vardiello, you won't tell anyone about this treasure, will you? For if you do, there'll be all sorts of rascals claiming it for their own, and we shall have nothing left. So, my clever son, can you keep a secret?"

"You can rely on me," he answered. "I'm not a fool like some people!"

But his shrewd mother was not so sure. "Be a good lad," she said, "and stand by the door. I'm expecting the milkman any minute. Watch out for him, will you?"

So Vardiello propped himself up against the door and watched.

But his mother went to the cupboard and filled her apron with

36

dried figs and raisins. Then she crept upstairs and quietly opened the window. She threw the figs and raisins out of the window by the handful.

Vardiello, down by the door, saw the raisins and figs falling from the sky.

"Oh, good!" he said, and he began to stuff them into his mouth. "Delicious!"

"Mother!" he called between mouthfuls. "It's raining raisins and figs. Come quickly and bring bowls and baskets to collect them."

His mother, however, pretended not to hear and did not answer, and Vardiello couldn't be bothered to fetch her. He just went on stuffing himself until he was fit to burst. Then off he went to bed. Of course he forgot about the milkman, but his mother was not too worried about that!

For a few days Vardiello kept his secret and told no one about the gold. But one day, as he was walking along the road, he met two friends who were fighting about a gold coin they had found. Each one claimed to have seen it first and was not going to give it up.

"I couldn't be bothered quarreling over one gold coin," said Vardiello.

"Is that so?" said one. "Of course, a fool like you wouldn't even recognize a gold coin if he saw one!"

"That's not true," said Vardiello. "One day I found a jar full of gold coins."

Now the secret was out. In no time, everyone in Naples knew that Vardiello had found a jar full of gold.

Soon, all sorts of rascals went hurrying along to the local judge, claiming to be the rightful owners. They had "lost it" or "hidden it" or "it had been stolen" from them. So, at last, the judge ordered an investigation into the whole affair, and Vardiello and his mother had to be questioned.

The day came, and the first question the judge asked was, "Who found the gold?"

"My son, sir," answered the widow. "At least my son, Vardiello, says he found some gold. He is a good lad, Your Honor, but I think that I should warn you that he does get rather strange ideas in his head and says some foolish things."

"Well, my lad," said the judge, "tell me about this gold."

"It was like this. One day I killed the hen and smashed her eggs. I chased the dog who stole the hen. I filled the cellar with good red wine. And *then* I ate poison. But alas! I didn't die."

"Yes, yes," said the judge, "but what about the gold?"

"It was like this. Next day I sold some cloth to a silent man. And the next day he refused to pay me—because he wasn't real."

"Yes, yes, yes," said the judge impatiently. "Now tell me about the gold."

"Well," said Vardiello, "I threw a brick at the silent man. I smashed

him right open. And there was a jar of gold inside his stomach."

"I see," said the judge. "Can you tell me when this happened?"

"Oh, yes!" cried Vardiello. "I'll never forget that day! *It was the day it rained raisins and figs!*"

"*The day it rained raisins and figs!*" said the judge. "That is too much!"

Then he turned to the widow and he said, "I see what you mean about strange ideas. It is obvious that there never was a jar of gold. Your son has a very vivid imagination."

So Vardiello's shrewd mother kept the treasure, and the two of them were able to live together very comfortably. In their garden there were always many hens and chicks, while in the cupboard there was always an abundance of raisins and figs and walnut creams!

THE DRAGON KING'S PALACE

An Old Japanese Story

he young fisherman, Urashima Taro, had been out all day fishing. On his way home he passed a gang of boys tormenting a turtle which they had caught.

"Hey!" he called to the boys. "That's no way to treat the creature. Why don't you let him go back to the sea where he came from?"

They ignored him—until he put his hands in his pocket and pulled out a few coins. Then they eagerly took the money and cheerfully gave up their victim.

Taro picked up the turtle, carried it to the edge of the sand, and let it swim away.

The next day, as always, he rose at dawn and was soon well out to sea, fishing all alone. Then he heard what he thought was his name called from a great distance, "Urashima-San! Urashima-San!"

"That's strange," he thought, since there was no

ship in sight and certainly no one appeared to be in the water nearby.

But then he noticed a turtle swimming alongside his boat.

"Did you call, Turtle-San?" asked Taro politely.

"Yes, I want to thank you for saving my life yesterday," said the turtle.

"Come aboard!" said Taro, and the turtle heaved itself up into the boat and lay peacefully in the sun.

For a while Taro quietly went on with his fishing. Then the turtle said, "You deserve to be rewarded for your kindness. Have you ever visited the palace of the Dragon King?"

"Never," said Taro. "All the fishermen talk about it, yet no one has ever been there."

"Then come with me," said the turtle. "I'll take you there, if you lift me over the side and climb on my back."

So Taro lifted the turtle back into the sea and clambered onto his hard shell. For a long time he clung to the turtle as it swam along on the surface of the water. Then, suddenly, it dived and he found himself submerged in the deep blue water. It took him by surprise, and he did not even have time to take a deep breath, but he discovered that he could breathe quite easily under the sea and he was able to admire the scenery as they sped along.

It was a long voyage, but they came, at last, to a great gateway. At the command of the turtle the gates swung open, and they swam into a courtyard. Before them was a palace made of corals and sea gems, which shone through the gloom of the deep. Surrounding the palace were four gardens, one for each of the four seasons, so that the king might enjoy spring blossoms, summer fruits, autumn colors, and snow and ice, simply by moving from one garden to the next.

The turtle let Taro down and told him to go wherever he wished. So he wandered about for a long time, wondering at everything he saw. Then he came to an inner garden where Otohiene, the daughter of the Dragon King, sat singing to herself. Taro fell to his knees and put his head on the ground before her, for he had never seen such splendor and majesty before.

"Stand up, Urashima-San," said the princess. "Welcome to my palace."

"Most humble thanks, Your Highness."

"No, do not thank me. It is I who thank you. You saved me from death. I am the turtle, and because of your goodness I am now restored to my true self."

Then she took him by the hand and led him through the gardens. She had food and wine brought to them, and they sat together and ate while fish made music and lobsters danced. The two had much

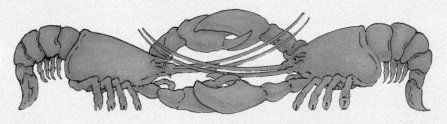

to talk about, and they found that they wished to spend the rest of their lives together. The Dragon King had no objection to a marriage, and they were wed amid joy and merriment.

All went well for some time. Then, one morning, Taro awoke from a dream of his home on dry land—of his mother and father. How strange that he had not thought of them before! His face was wet with tears of longing and regret. The princess, his wife, was distressed to see his grief. He told her that he wished to visit his parents before they were too old, and that he must go at once before they died. Although sad to see him leave so soon, she could not hinder him from visiting his parents.

"Go and visit them, my husband," she said, "but do not forget your wife while you are away, for she loves you dearly. Here, take this little box. Think of me whenever you look at it, for it contains something very precious. But you must never open it. If you do so, great sorrow will come upon you."

So Urashima Taro sadly left his wife and went with the little box to the gates of the palace. There, a giant turtle met him and carried him on its back to land.

When Taro saw the mountains of his homeland his heart filled with joy. He waded quickly ashore and looked around him. On the sand stood an old man with a bent back, and with a pang he thought that it looked like his father. He ran forward to greet him but found that it was a stranger.

So he took the path to his father's cottage. How strange! It was gone! Where it had stood there was now a large house. He knocked on the door and a strange man opened it.

"Sir," he said, "can you tell me the whereabouts of the family of Urashima Taro, the fisherman?"

"What are you talking about? Those people died three hundred years ago."

"But I am Urashima Taro," said the young man.

"Don't talk nonsense," said the man. "They say that Urashima Taro, the fisher-boy, disappeared at sea one day long ago. It was my great-grandfather who bought his house and pulled it down to build this one. Is this a joke or something?"

"It is no joke. I am Urashima Taro, and I'm seventeen years old."

"Urashima Taro has been gone three hundred years," said the man. "Go visit the priest. It is written in the temple records."

Taro walked sadly away. All around him he saw that the old familiar things had gone. There was not one person whom he recognized, not even one house that he remembered. What he thought was a period of a few weeks away from home had been three hundred years.

He went back to the water's edge and sat on the sand. He looked into the water, down toward the palace which he had left. How could he ever get back there again?

In his arms he still carried the little box which the princess, his wife, had given him. Would this help him to return? She had tied it up with a golden cord. But she had warned him never to open it. Perhaps she did not realize what dire trouble he would be in.

"I don't know what else to do, my dearest wife," he said out loud. "Forgive me if I disobey you."

He put the little box on the sand, untied the cord, and lifted the lid. It was empty. All that came out was a sweet-smelling perfume that drifted past and was gone.

He sat on the sand without moving. Slowly his strength and his youth ebbed away. His eyes dimmed. Wrinkles spread over his face, and his hair turned as white as snow. His body shrank, and with a soft cry he fell forward and lay still.

The next day, on the way to the boats, fishermen discovered the body of an old man lying on the shore. Beside him lay a golden box.

"Is this the person who came to your door yesterday?" asked one.

"No, that was a fine young man. Do you know he tried to tell me that he was Urashima Taro! How's that for a joke!"

BABA YAGA'S
SEVEN
SWAN-GEESE

An Old Tale from Russia

Once, and long ago it was, Katya was left to mind her fat baby brother while her parents went to sow the fields. She put the baby down on the grass and ran off to chat with her friends.

No sooner had Katya left than a flock of swan-geese, seven great white birds, swooped from the skies and carried off the little boy.

Katya heard his squeals, and at first she didn't know what to do. She ran about weeping and calling and searching for her brother, but he was nowhere. Then, far away, where the sky and fields met, she saw the swan-geese strung across the blueness like a strand of thick white yarn. She knew then what had become of her brother. The swan-geese had stolen him.

Watching the birds and stumbling across the fields

of newly tilled earth, she followed their flight. She ran until she was breathless. Then the birds dropped from sight below the horizon, and Katya bumped into an oven. An oven in a field? She was too distressed to be amazed and cried out, "Oven! Please, Oven, tell me where the swan-geese have flown."

"Eat one of my rye loaves, then I shall tell what I know," answered the oven.

"I couldn't do that! At my father's house I only eat fine wheaten loaves, never black bread. Besides, I must find my

brother." Katya was too distracted to be mindful of the oven's request.

She ran on, out of the field to an apple tree growing at the meadow's edge. "Apple Tree! Please, Apple Tree, tell me where the swan-geese have flown."

"Eat one of my wild apples, then I shall tell what I know," answered the apple tree.

"I couldn't do that! At my father's house I only eat garden-sweet apples. Besides, I must find my brother."

Katya ran faster over the meadow's springy green grass and she met a cow. "Cow! Please, Cow, tell me where the swan-geese have flown."

"Drink some of my sour milk, then I shall tell what I know."

"I couldn't do that! At my father's house I only drink fresh sweet milk. Besides, I must find my brother."

Once more Katya ran. She ran into darkness, thick and shadowy, through which a light flashed from the window of a hut, a vile eyesore of a place which perched high off the ground, atop four clawed chicken legs. Slowly, eerily, the hut circled round and round, flashing the swinging light. It lit up Baba Yaga, another vile eyesore—bone-thin hooked nose and long pointed chin; glinting never-still frog-eyes, forever rolling, forever spying and prying; greedy mouth, thick of lips and dribblesome; and hair streaked and bristling like a deserted bird's nest. Oh, she was something to see, and there she sat spinning and in need of a scrubbing and combing. At her feet sat Katya's little brother, playing with five silver balls!

Katya's heart leaped with joy, then thudded with fear. "Good evening, Granny!" she called. Oh, she was much braver than she felt.

"Now what brings you here, Little One?" cackled Baba Yaga, hobbling to the door.

"My dress is wet with dew. May I dry it by your fire?" Katya asked primly, never mentioning her brother. She knew that the old witch would enchant them both if she were crossed in any way.

"Dry your dress, you shall," honeyed Baba Yaga, showing her long green and yellow teeth. "Come to the fire and I'll fetch water to make you some tea." She handed her spindle to Katya, then sprang from the door, calling, "Spin for me, Child, while I'm gone."

Katya began to spin as if she couldn't stop. Her brother played as if he couldn't stop. And there they were, half-bewitched in the still quiet hut, when a mouse crept from its hole under the stove. "Give me some porridge, Katya! There! From the pot on the stove," it squeaked.

"Of course!" she said and spooned out porridge for the mouse.

As the mouse ate it said, "Baba Yaga is in the bathhouse, Katya. She is boiling water in the kettle, Katya, to steam you and wash you, then roast you in the oven, Katya. She will eat you up, then ride the sky on your bones, Katya!"

Katya almost fainted and only just heard the mouse advise, "Put your brother on your hip, Katya, and run for home. I will spin rope for you."

In a daze, Katya picked up her brother, jumped from the hut, and sped away.

From the bathhouse, Baba Yaga screamed, "Are you spinning, dear Child?"

"I am spinning, Granny!" shrieked the mouse.

Nodding her head, licking her lips, Baba Yaga stoked the fire, and the kettle bubbled and steamed. She clanged on its lid, sprang into the house, and found her prize was gone. And the fat boy-babe! And the mouse... into its hole. The spindle lay on the floor in a tangle of rope.

"Eeeeee!" Baba Yaga squawked. "Swan-geese, fly! Capture Katya! Capture the boy! Swan-geese, fly!"

Wings flapped, and seven wildly honking swan-geese flew, flew low, seeking Katya. She heard their beating wings and called across the meadow, "Help me, please, Cow!"

"Drink some of my sour milk," said the cow.

Katya swallowed a choking, cloying, sour mouthful, then another and another, and the cow nudged the children down beside her, hiding them in her bulky shadow as the swan-geese winged overhead, unable to see their prey.

Now Katya ran to the apple tree, but the swan-geese swerved, doubling back towards her. "Help me, please, Apple Tree!" she begged.

"Eat one of my wild apples."

Katya chewed into the bitter apple, crunching, shuddering, swallowing mouthfuls as the apple tree stooped, spreading out leafy branches which covered the children like sheltering arms, and once more the swan-geese missed their prey.

And once more Katya ran on. Her arms ached with the weight of her brother. Her legs slowed with pain. A stitch stabbed sharply at her side. Somehow, she limped on, but the swan-geese honked, screamed, and screeched above her head.

Katya made for the oven. "Please, oh please, help me!"

"Eat one of my loaves."

Gasping, Katya bit into the crusted, dusty-dry, dark loaf. It cut and scratched her mouth, but she swallowed mouthful after mouthful, and the oven pushed the children through its door and clanged it shut.

Katya heard the swan-geese screaming, thrashing the oven with their wings, clawing and pecking it, bullying it to give up the children. And they attacked the oven until at last Baba Yaga whistled them home.

Katya tumbled out of the oven and carried her little brother to their house. No sooner were they settled inside than their parents came in with hugs and kisses for the children. Then there were pancakes with sugar and cream for supper.

As for Baba Yaga, she went without supper and no doubt is still hungry, because swan-geese gave up stealing children long, long ago.